The Wonderful History and Surprising Prophecies of Mother Shipton

THE WONDERFUL HISTORY AND SURPRISING PROPHECIES OF Mother SHIPTON.

Printed for the *Travelling Stationers*.

THE WONDERFUL
HISTORY
And surprising
PROPHECIES
OF
Mother SHIPTON.

CHAP. I. *Of her Birth.*

MOther Shipton (as all Histories agree) was a Yorkshire Woman, the particular Place is very much disputed. Because several Towns have pretended to the Honour of her Birth, but the most credible Opinions ascribe it to the Town of Knaresborough, near the Dropping-well in the County aforesaid. Concerning her Pedigree or Parentage, there are likewise various Reports, some say her Father was a Necromancer, and that he had Skill in the Black Art, whereby it became entail

entail'd upon her by Birth: But the common Story, which I shall follow, is, that she never had a Father of human race, but was begot as the Welch Prophet Merlin was of old by the Phantasm of Apollo, or some wanton ariel Dæmon in the following surprising Manner.

Her Mother, whom some Records call Agatha, and others Ematha, was left an Orphan about the Age of sixteen very poor, and much troubled with that grievous, but common Disease called Idleness; and by some Sloth; as she was once upon a Time sitting bemoaning herself on a shady Bank by the Highway Side, a Spirit appear'd unto her in the Shape of a handsome young Man, and smiling on her, pretty Maid, quoth he, why dost thou sit so sad. thou art not hold enough to have thy Head pestered with the Cares of the World: Prithee tell me thy Business, and doubt not but I will help thee out of all thy Troubles. The Maid, (for Maids were in those Days at her age,) casting up her Eyes, and

no

not suspecting a Devil, hid in so comely a Countenance related to him her Wants, and that she knew not how to live; Pish, said he, be rul'd by me, and thou shall never lack, she hearing him promise so fairly, told him she would; and thereupon to draw her in by Degrees to Destruction, first tempted her to Fornication, but his Touches, as she afterwards confessed to the Midwife, were as cold as Snow, from this Time forward, she was commonly visited once a Day by her hellish Gallant, and never wanted Money as she swept the House she constantly found some Piece; as Nine-pences, Quarter-Thirteen-pence-Half-pennies; and the like, sufficient to supply all her Occasions.

CHAP. II.

Agatha proved with Child: and how she fitted the severe Justice, and what happened at her Delivery.

THE Neighbours observing Agatha without any Employ to live

so handsomely, wondered exceedingly how she came by it, but were more surprized shortly afterwards, when they perceived her with Child, which she could not hide. For before her Delivery, she was as big as if she had gone with half a Dozen Children at once, whereupon she was carried before a Justice, who threatened, and chided her for Incontinency, but he was soon silenced, for his Wife and all his Family being present, Agatha said to him aloud, Mr. Justice, how gravely you talk, and yet the Truth is, your Worship is not altogether free, for here stands two of your Servant Wenches, that are both at this Time with Child by you, pointing to them severally with her Finger, at which both himself and the two Girls were so blank, that his Wife plainly saw what she said was true, and therefore fell upon the two Harlots like a Fury, and all Mr. Justice and the Constable could do, was not enough to keep the Peace, and the whole was in such Confusion that Agatha for that Time was dismiss'd, miss'd, and soon after was brought to Bed in the Month of July, in the fourth Year of the Reign of King Henry the Seventh, which was in the Year of our Lord 1488. Her Travel was very grievous, and a most terrible Clap of Thunder happened just as she was delivered of this strange Birth, which afterwards was so famous by the Name of Mother Shipton: For could the Tempest affright the Woman more than the prodigious Physiognomy of the Child. The Body was long and very big boned great gogling Eyes very sharp and fiery; a Nose of unproportionable Length, having in it many Crooks and Turnings, adorned with great Pimples, which like Vapour of Brimstone, gave such a Lustre in the Night, that her Nurse needed no Candle to dress her by: And besides this uncouth Shape, it was observed, that as she was born she fell a laughing and grinning after a geering Manner, and immediately after the Tempest ceased.

CHAP.

CHAP. III.

THE Child being thus brought into the World under such strange Circumstances, was, tho' not without some Opposition, order'd to be christened by the Abbot of Beverley which was performed by the Name of Ursula Soathiel, for the latter her Mother's maiden Sir-Name: And as for Shipton it was the Name of her Husband, whom she afterwards married, as will appear in the Sequel of this History; and in this Particular most of the Authors I have read, have been greatly mistaken. But to proceed, when she was about two Years old, her Mother coming to be sensible of her Evil, holding Correspondence with a wicked Spirit, apply'd herself to several religious Men of Note in those Times, by whose grave Advice she grew truly penitent, and according to the Fashion of that Age's Devotion, put out her Child with a Piece of Money to a Friend, and so spent the Remainder of her Days in the famous
Convent

Convent of St. Bridget's, Nottingham, in Prayers and Tears, and other Acts of Pennance, to expatiate the Wickedness of her Youth; but wonderful it is to relate the Troubles the Nurse to whom she was put, had; her Father the foul Fiend, is reported several Times to have visited her, particularly one Day the Nurse having been abroad, when she returned, found her Door open, whereupon, fearing that she was robbed, she called three or four Neighbours and their Wives to go into the House with her; but before they had got into the Entry they heard a strange Noise, as if there had been a Thousand Carts in Concert; which so dismayed them, that they all ran towards the Door, endeavouring to get out again, but in vain; for every one of them had got Yoakes on their Necks, that they could not possibly return; but soon after the Yoaks fell off, and then a Colt-staff was laid on two of the Men's Shoulders, upon which an old Woman presented herself stark naked, sometimes hanging by by the Heels, sometimes by the Toes, then by the Middle, with divers other Postures, while the Women having all their Coats turn'd over their Ears, exposed their Shame to public Views, and so continued till a Friar accidentally came to the House and suddenly released them; and as the Child was taken out of the Cradle, it could not be found, till at last one of the Company saw it stand naked, sitting astride upon the Iron to which the Pot-hooks were fastened, whence they took it down without the least hurt. And so far from being frightened, that it seemed by its agreeable Smiles to be very well pleased at these strange Exploits.

CHAP. IV.

Several merry Pranks play'd by Mother Shipton on such as abused her.

AS Ursula grew to riper Years she was often affronted by reason of her Deformity; but she never fail'd to be revenged on those that

that did it. One Day the Chief of the Parish being a merry Meeting she coming thither occasionally on an Errand, some of them abused her, by calling her the Devil's Bastard, and Hag-face, and the like, whereat she went away grumbling, but so ordered her Affairs, that when they sat down to Dinner, one of the principal Yeomen that thought himself spruce and fine, had in an Instant his Ruff (which in those Days they wore) pull'd off, and the Seat of a House of Office clapt in it's Place: He that sat next him, burst out in a Laughter at the Sight thereof, but was served little better: For his Hat was invisibly conveyed away, and the Pan of a Close-stool which stood in the next Room put on instead thereof: Besides this a modest young Gentlewoman that sat at the Table, at the same Time looking at these two Objects of Mirth, endeavoured all she could to refrain laughing, but could not! And withal continued breaking Wind backward, for above a Quarter of an Hour together, like so many
Broad-

Broad-Sides in a Sea-Fight, which made all the Company laugh so extreamly, that the Master of the House being alarmed below therewith, and desirous to share with his Guests in their Mirth, came running up the Stairs as fast as his Legs would carry him, but going to enter the Door, he could not, and no Wonder, for he had a swinging Pair of Horns fixed on his Head; so many of the Company being surprizingly adorned and afflicted, it threw the whole Meeting into the greatest Consternation and Amazement, lest any more should be tormented after this uncommon Manner: And whilst they were gazing on one another, as more than Half distracted, they were all reduced to the same Condition they were in at first, after which followed a Noise as if more than a Hundred Persons were a laughing together, but nothing was seen, neither was it possible for them to account for the sudden Alteration.

CHAP.

CHAP. V.

Ursula married a young Man named Toby Shipton, and strangely discovered a Thief.

OUR Ursula was now arrived at the 24th Year of her Age, and although she was none of the prettiest Maids in the Town, yet she longed for a Husband as much as any of them and at last obtained her Desire; whether she used any Love-Powder, or Charms to enamour him; or whether the Hopes of getting some Money, which she was reported to have, though no Body could tell how she should come by it, caused him to court her (there are some Men that would not only marry the Devil's Daughter, but his Dam too for Money) a Sweetheart she had, and we are told his Name was Toby Shipton, by Trade a Carpenter, to whom she was shortly after married, and very comfortably they lived together, but never had any Children. It happened about a

Month

Month after her Marriage, one of her Neighbours leaving her Door carelesly open, loſt a new Smock and Petticoat, which was ſtole away while ſhe was telling a Goſſip's Tale of an Hour long, at the next Door, whither ſhe went to fetch Fire, which ſad Misfortune much troubled her, ſhe made her Moan to Mother Shipton, who did not go about it like our ſilly Conjurers, with their Schemes and Figures, to give a blind Deſcription of ſhe knew not what, but told her plainly ſuch a Woman by Name had ſtolen the Things; adding that ſhe would make her reſtore them with Shame to her, and ſo indeed ſhe did; for the next Market-Day before all the People, the Woman could not avoid putting on the Smock over her other Cloaths, and the Petticoat in her Hand, and ſo marched thro' a Crowd in the Market-Place, dancing all the Way and ſinging theſe Words,

'Tis true I ſtole my Neighbour's
Smock and Coat.
I am a ſorry Thief and here ſhow't.
And

And so when she came to the Owner, she pulled off the Smock and gave it her with a reverend Courtesy, and with great Sorrow, and seeming Repentance, begged Forgiveness for her wicked Doings, assuring her she would reform from her wicked Ways, and be more honest and diligent for the future.

CHAP. IV.
Her Prophecy against Cardinal Wolsey.

BY these, and several the like Exploits, Mother Shipton had got a Name far and near for a cunning Woman or a Woman of Foresight, so that her Words were counted Oracles, nor did she meddle only with Private Persons, but also with Persons of the greatest Quality; among whom at that Time was Cardinal Wolsey when it was reported that he intended to live at YORK, she publickly said he should never come thither! which coming to his Ear, and being offended at it, he caused three Lords to go to her, who came disguised to Ringhouse near York, where they took a
Guide

Guide, and came to Mother Shipton and knocking at her Door, she cried out, come in Mr. Beasly, and those noble Lords with you; which much surprized them, that she should know them, and when they came in, she called each of them by their Names and treated them with Ale and Cakes, whereupon, said one of them, if you knew our Errand, you would not make so much of us: You said, the Cardinal should never see York. No, said she, I said he might see York, but never come at it: Well, said one of the Lords, when he does come thou shall be burnt; then taking the Handkerchief from her Head, says she, if this burn I shall burn, and immediately flung it into the Fire before them where after laying a Quarter of an Hour, she took it out again, not so much as singed: Hereupon one of the Lords asked her what she thought of him? My Lord, said she, the Time will come when your Grace will be as low as I am, which was very true for shortly after he was beheaded:

Nor

Nor was her Speech of the Cardinal's less verified; for he coming to Cawood, went to the Top of the Tower, and ask'd where York was, which being shewn him, he enquired how far it was thither? For quoth he, there is a Witch said I never should see York, no, says one present, your Eminence was misinformed, she said you would see it, but never come at it. Then he vows to burn her when he came there, which was about 8 Miles distant, but an Express overtook him on the Road, which informed him the King immediately wanted his Counsel, so that he suddenly turned back to wait on his Majesty, and being taken ill upon the Road, he died of a violent Looseness at Westminster.

CHAP. VII.

Some other Prophecies of Mother Shipton, relating to those Times.

AT divers other Times when Persons of Quality came to visit her

she

she used to divert them with several uncommon Fancies, and amongst the rest of her Amusements, she delivered the following Prophecies to them:

FIRST PROPHECY.

Before Ouse-Bridge and Trinity-Church meet they shall build in the Day and it shall fall in the Night, until they get the highest Stone of Trinity Church, and the lowest Stone of Ouse-Bridge.

This truly came to pass for Trinity Steeple in York was blown down with a Tempest, and Ouse-bridge broke down with a Flood; and what they did in the Day-time in repairing the Bridge, was washed down in the night till at last they laid the highest Stone for the Foundation of the Bridge, which being cemented with a different Mortar than what was used before resisted the Force of the Water, and made a good Foundation.

SECOND PROPHECY.

A Time shall happen when a Ship shall

shall come sailing up the Thames, till it come against London; and the Master of the Ship shall weep, and the Mariners of the Ship shall ask why he weeps since he made so good a Voyage! and he shall say, Ah? what a goodly City this was, none in the World comparable to it, and now there is scarce Drink for our Money.

EXPLANATION.

These last Words were sadly verified after the dreadful fire of London, 1666. When there was not a House left all along the Thames Side, from the Tower to the Temple. As for the Words before they being darkly delivered, he that both hides and discovers all Things shall bring the Matters signified to Light.

CHAP. VII.

Her Prophecies in Verse to the Abbot of Beverly.

THE Abbot of Beverly paying her a Visit one Day, told her, That
as

as he had found several Things that she had formerly said to be exactly true, so he was persuaded that she was not ignorant in which for the future were to ensue; and therefore requested her to impart some of her Fore-knowledge unto him, for which Favour, tho' more than his Deserts could command, yet should he never want a Tongue to acknowledge nor a Heart to endeavour a Requital for so great an Obligation. Mr. Abbot says she leave off complimenting. I am an old Woman, I will neither flatter nor be flattered by any, yet shall I answer your Desires, and therefore she did in mistick Verses discover unto him the greatest Accidents that have happened in England from that Day to this; as the following Explanation of her Prophecies will more abundantly shew.

PROPHECY.

Whene'er the Cow doth ride the Bull,
O Priest I say, beware thy Skull.

EXPLA-

EXPLANATION.

By the Cow was meant Henry VIII. who gave the Cow in his Arms, as the Earl of Richmond, and the Bull betokens Madam Ann of Bullogne, not only as to the firſt Syllable of her Name, but becauſe her Father gave the Black Bull's Head in his Creſt; and when the King married her, immediately followed the Diſſolution of Monaſteries and ſore Reſtraints laid upon Prieſts.

PROPHECY.

For a ſweet pious Prince make Room,
And in each Kirk prepare a Broom.

EXPLANATION.

This is meant of King Edward VI. in whoſe Time the Proteſtant Religion was eſtabliſhed, and the Popiſh Superſtition ſwept out of the Kirk, an old Word uſed ſtill in Scotland, for the Church.

PRO-

PROPHECY.

Alecto next assumes the Crown,
And streams of Blood run swiftly down.

EXPLANATION.

These Lines decipher Queen Mary, called Alecto, the Name of one of the Furies, for her Cruelty to the Protestants, of whom great Numbers in her Reign were burnt in Smithfield.

PROPHECY.

A Maiden Queen full many a Year,
Shall England's warlike Sceptre bear.

EXPLANATION.

Spoken of Queen Elizabeth, who reigned greatly beloved by her Subjects and dreaded by all her Enemies above forty Years.

PROPHECY.

The Western Monarch's wooden horses
Shall be destroy'd by old Drake's forces

EXPLANATION.

The King of Spain's mighty Navy in 1588 destroyed by the English Fleet under Captain Drake.

PROPHECY.

The Northern Lion over Tweed,
The maiden Queen shall next succeed,
To join in one two mighty States,
And then shall Janus shut his Gates.

EXPLANATION.

This relates to King James, who having been many Years King of Scotland, the Crown of England by Queen Elizabeth's Death fell to him, whereupon he came over Tweed to take up his Residence here, and so joined the two King dom doms under one Government. And as for Janus shutting his Gates; you must know Janus was one of the Heathen Gods that had a Temple at Rome, the Gates of which were never shut but in Times of Peace.

THIS famous Prophetess continued several Years esteemed as the Sybil or Oracle of those Times. At last arriving to threescore and thirteen years of age, she found the Time in her black Book of Destiny approaching, wherein she must give a final adieu to the World which she foretold to a Day to divers People. And at the Hour predicted having taken solemn Leave of all her Friends, laid her down on her Bed and died.

FINIS.

Lightning Source UK Ltd.
Milton Keynes UK
UKHW020646090223
416652UK00001B/4